Control Bird Alt Delete

Control Bird Alt Delete

by Alexandria Peary

UNIVERSITY OF IOWA PRESS, *Iowa City*

University of Iowa Press, Iowa City 52242
Copyright © 2014 by Alexandria Peary
www.uiowapress.org
Printed in the United States of America

Design by Barbara Haines

The University of Iowa Press is a member of Green Press Initiative and is committed to preserving natural resources.

Printed on acid-free paper

ISBN-13: 978-1-60938-245-2
ISBN-10: 1-60938-245-5
LCCN: 2013950696

To my parents

CONTENTS

Fridge

From the filled-in cellar hole
from the underlined place
in a gathering of birches
rises a 1950s jay-blue
fridge shaking its ratty cord,
a cow skull in a grass skirt,

Bantam-lord of the yellowed hip
bones of dairy cows, of old oil cans,
up to its waist in a crumbling
leaf-mold of -pedic, Thermosol,
-aire Esso, a Deluxe, Sleepwell

hooking up to the dreaming place.
From the filled-in cellar hole
(where the apothecary,
where the pastor's house
had been) I dug up a sliver
of a button, bone, *whereas*
from the leaf-rot of Flynntan
eok Mill Amos, -tech, analogic
around the mills like a moat,

From Universal Warehouse, from
the GE plant Kodak and the rubble
of the Necco candy factory
my brother *becomes an engineer*
finds a tiny blue bottle
as small as my daughter.

Post No Bills with Fridge Magnets
on its slippery door, the fridge
is keeper of yellowed food,
spiders, recluse, Brown
shot-up Pepsi cans,
a 30-year-old Duncan Hines
cake mix on its shelf,

sends out the call to dinner
across the fields: intact Whirl
pool opening and closing,
new Maytag, Samsung
in small houses each
set atop its own underlining
It's time to stop digging.

hooking up to the dreaming place
pale poles of trees
Plugs himself in.

Like That

An enormous snow-covered branch
is threatening the living room.

An enormous tanned branch
with snow like heaps of table linens
or the clumped, white language of animals
juts into the living room.

A pile of dead oak leaves stands
in the doorway. If I walk into the room,
snow will ruin the somber furniture.

Across the dining room table
and under the cheap glass chandelier,
across the empty space for the Sunday roast
and the doily, my sister, brother and I are cross-country skiing

when a giant embroidered
chickadee
crosses the room
putting a word in my ear.

Deconstructing New England

Toss in some wavy lines, an equal sign, and a squiggle,
then a lilac log, boulders with faces, a few phrases
like rock walls, twin marks from wagon wheels on granite.
The tell-tale lilacs give away the cellar hole:
magnetic lilacs, like nineteenth-century girls
in pinafores and blossom sprays, stationed
beside their no-longer houses. They look about to sing.
Banana curls. Purple ribbons tying their waists.
And boulders in the woods act as billboards
interrupted by an enormous Mont Blanc fountain pen, lounging
like an alligator. It intrudes. Comes out of my present
time. No. Be less. It's a Bic ballpoint. Bleached by deletion,
"By the middle of the nineteenth century, when de
forestation reached its peak, more than half
of New England's native forests"—according to Robert M. Thorson,
Stone by Stone—"as much as 80 percent in the heavily settled
parts of southern New England—had been cut down,"
"replaced with 'open space,'" the autumn foliage
is paint-by-number and different tabs throughout
                    are half-finished murals
of a single type of tree in a single time of year.
Here's the place where someone w/ a pewter spoon kneeled
to plant the Lady's Slippers that still appear,
and the mushrooms like a stack of dinner plates
that run up the side of a rotting tree.
Here's the fallen-in deer stand
and the apple tree among maples making fruit for deer.
Outside the woods, the puff of dust on the road
where the school bus used to stop.

Outside is the failure to stay in touch
or, really, to ever be in touch. I didn't
ever know them (my neighbors) well.
In winter you are handed a white tray
with a few tiny rock walls, short lines drawn with a ruler,
an indent for where a cellar hole could be
a hyperlink to once go once more to the lake
and told to go at it, go play.

Oh, Massachusetts

I pick up the border
of Massachusetts—and drop it
I twang, twang, twang it,
the wavy line, the magnetic line
the ins and outs of it
that make a profile,
inlets and vestibules,
estuaries and the entrance
to a McDonald's.
After a few seconds,
the cove and a bar code
of poplar trees stop moving.
I pick up the border
of Massachusetts—and drop it
I thrum, thrum, thrum it,
the lyric mile,
poetic lines like peninsulas, jetties, long reaches, sand bars in
     octometer, calcified prose
with revolving towns,
bead cities
shiny with information
& after miles of generalities
the door knob to the women's restroom in a Starbucks,
the wicker mail box in the lobby
15 Arlington, Apartment 27.
I pick up Route 3, a junction,
and Walnut Path and drop them drop them,
and the end of the line
ekes out fife music,

murmur of the militia,
construction sounds of the new museum
wing, then falls silent.
While the heron on one leg in the bay
like a swizzler stick
like a lawn flamingo in Leominster
watches, the border slams
the ground one more time,
making the granite floor
in the baby's room rattle,
I could break the prose across my knee
and make a 3-lined shelf
for the state bird, flower, tree,
the Mayflower, I-Max, and the brick factories,
but I strum, I strum,
strum, strum it,
and a yellow river
dribbles down my chest
—a passing lane
of crèche paper, party streamer
from the jade cave:
I am only a mile from my heart.

Lilacs as Chart

The purple & white bars
rising and falling
are on mute
around the cellar hole

on mute
the long and short
eeee   ee
rising and falling

near the word count
beside the cellar hole

those electronic and
embroidered
e's

of the purple & white bars
rising and falling
in the dappled place

are joined now by the neutral,
black, and tan bars
that are on hold
in a flesh-tones graph,
the long and short *o* sounds

like paused petals

in the dappled place
in the spliced woods

strips of
birches and poplar

with grooves from
wagon wheels in the granite
near the double-decker
boulder:

it takes a decade
in the granite woods
for the petals to
descend, dove
-colored sounds,
lilacs
in September.

Lilacs

I take the letter *e* out of all the lilacs
along with any parts that occur in summer
from a paperback novel that I pull from a swan-shaped basket
for magazines found at Goodwill:
and I will not think about
will not think about the show
about the road bending all over the place,
or the pasture plowed into white.

Putty and puce *e*'s with purple hyphens,
electronic and embroidered *e*'s
ones found in stacks near cellar holes
in the woods made from splices,
and from the novel, contrails of dialog and blurry furniture,
no, I will forget the vertical horizon
the painting of an immense field plowed white
that replaced the Sears painting over the sofa,
and the coin-operated boxes starting to move.

I make the *e*'s perform
like emoticons of grumpy old men
in a pyramid of cheerleaders
and the piece with a shadow of a woman's hat
interlocks with the grasshopper
on a bed. Happy faces have been drawn
on the dew. *I hear the word "gramophone."*
I find a vase covered in bumper stickers
and Subject lines. *It's a hat box*
on the guest bed and a locust.

A breeze has been sprayed with lavender Febreeze,
a lengthy passage has been written in amethyst and green
when the faces start falling, this stack of faces
falling, rising and falling within one face,
one face that contains a 100, falling,
a purple & white mist, a red-white-and-blue mist,
I will not think about the human mist.

A Decal of Lilacs

A decal of lilacs
is near a rock wall
given as a graduation present
(walls came in pewter, silver, bronze)
(I selected pewter).

The decal was on the same rack
as the Keep On Truckin' thumb
which knows the Charleston Chew,
the Zig-Zag rolling papers,
which knows the orange workman's gloves,
sticky green Life Savers,
not to mention the scratch 'n sniff unicorn
that eluded inventory
by keeping one hoof in
the piano music playing backwards,

but more often than not, lilacs
are filed phenomeno
logically after cellar holes
(where swing set once stood) (outhouse)
(cobalt blue bottles) (unearthed Tupperware).
I thought about us walking the Old Post Road
at night in spring, putting our heads
together like the trees up ahead,
cellar holes in the woods on both sides.

At the graduation shop,
where it is May all year-round,

and two steel left hands are tying
rock walls over fields and woods,
a clashing sound when crossed with
faux stone walls in front of starter castles.

After the Flute Lesson, a Unicorn Rainbow Sticker
   Walking into the Birch Forest

The sense of lifting something—
a Magnetic swoosh, a Magnetic splash,
over an underlined place
that's on a tall, cool wall,
and setting it down
over an underlined place
where the swing set once stood,
between the brackets
and over a filled-in cellar hole.

Lifting that swoosh and setting it
on a tall, cool wall
which many people before you
touched with their foreheads

because of music that smelled like cedar.
After I dragged off
the cast-iron Buzz, a cast-iron Bang,
a Dusty click, a rusting Clack
came that music that smelled like cedar.

While between the poles
of a canopy bed
cumulous clouds were moving
between one quotation mark and the next
were moving between the poles
of the birches.

Bath Toys Sit in the Description

Bath toys sit in the description,
in the flat-iron reflecting pool
in the colorlessness of underlining,
alphabets and people who expand in water:
astronauts and little children,
men made entirely of denim.

In the clear pool of my inspection,
The People I Want to Be in the Next Life.
A woman in chinos walking the dog.
Two friends out speed-walking,
one carrying a French Vanilla coffee.
Anyone who eats instant oatmeal, Cup o'.
The truck driver, smoking, the early morning, WBAK.
The white paneled van that delivers
something whose meaning you don't understand
in this tidal pool of reflection.

They are names on a key chain,
& an iris, a dove, a Peace Be With You
And Also With You

all on a great Swoop—
for Quik insertion in a portal.

The Lottery of Winged Leaves

A word falls down the side of the poem
through the wings and two-ton leaves
wingèd leaves nailed to the tenement green
A word falls thru the blocks of letters on the page
changing some, hitting others, denting one
as I use my tin paddle-wings. A pre-fix It falls

the way snow falls into the arms of the trees
the way an answer can fall into the hillside of YYY that awaits it
the way color is mixed with an emotion in autumn
and is used only at the top of trees. Look:
the color of my daughter at age two, then five
a waterproof yellow near the plus sign of the maple

the ping, ding, bam! in a tiny font
as pieces of words hit trash can lids and run-down cars
outside the Greens' tenement in the present blue
and several more life bars are used up.
How many life bars has this used up? A dotted line
dropping from a window on the side of the poem,

it takes eight seconds for it to fall, using paddle-wings
I steer around the hulks of words
How many bars can I add? As the trees go up and down
Squares of stories open *A woman in the room she writes*
A word falls through the neighborhood, the chalked-in lines
of white-veined *logos* and *pathos*,

ancient trees that have moved into the side street
of dusty boxes seen from overhead

—a car shop, a warehouse, thrift store, two bars
one with Lotto unplugged in the front window.
Using my paddle-wings, it takes several years for the word
to navigate trees, branches of ctrl alt del.

How sometimes whatever you say drops right
into place as indigo and red shreds at sunset,
How morning enters like a blue equation.
Look, there's the color of my daughter age two, then age 5.
At the outskirts of the city, in the flood zone,
the trees rising and falling, a mountain range = seven years.

Bird Saver

ONE TUBE OF BIRD SONG joins the next
pipes fill the room with random action,
follow each other around, link arms
shadowy vectors and ducts of half made-
out sounds right behind, following each other
under the ceiling fan in the rented room
over the mattress drifting above bed springs
as a dirty cloud, above the radiator that says,
quote cloud unquote.
                      On a room that wavers, darkens, will reset,
pipes that come in three colors—promenade,
hacking, and white listening—a listening-to-opera-while-
cooking-dinner-near-an-open-window-in-early-spring—
and the do-si-do is on the brite green lawn,
a wallpaper of blossoms in the window pane.
                      Unlike the view
into a room that gets periodically bricked over,
the villa with an urn of pitch-black flowers on a vine,
or the origami of other birds the Baltimore oriole
folded over the cardinal over the cedar waxwing
let's mate! let's mate! there's still room to think,
to move around the room under the pipes,
a wallpaper of blossoms in the window pane.
The fly carries around its action like a wire hat.

Surveillance meteor

The surveillance meteor hangs over a stone wall
at the back of an hour that never begins
that shares one side of a what's-red-and-black-all-over
field that has the scent of a new playing card
and a droopy tree, melting at the top,

across from the half hour
that will put a branch in my neck
and take another part from my side.
All of this is a block away from spring,
from the flings 'n flashes, the high banks of,
the rows and rows of farmer's nuptials,
foam trees hiding a tennis court,
the flowering door and the Private Entrance
that the meteor surveys.

A surveillance meteor hangs above the tree,
at the back of an hour that never begins,
ragged as a fruit pit. It is two years before my birth,
and I am standing in a fash
ionable overcoat, my roadster colored in after-the-fact
& parked outside the courtyard.
                    Several eclipses will settle in the tree.
A scarlet light is speaking from the top of the tree,
You will mix with the moneyed but
view love differently. The tree stubbed out.
The tree catching fire on top. The silvery name
scratched out. The silvery name added to the log of births.

The surveillance meteor is out dispersing
a gang of comets & a flea sun skateboarding
off the faux stone wall in front of the shoppes in the hamlet,
who are ricocheting above the fold in the monograph on summer,
around the gash in the valu
able etching of a hayfield
torn from the PVBLIC LIBRARY,
down the country lane of ash trees and a business sunset
while the stone wall continues into the next four days

until a door opens in the mural,
the lower half a painted rock wall & butterflies & cornflowers
& morning glories, onto the manager's hidden room
(the manager is out dispersing the Comets & Sun),
the hidden room that opens in the middle of the sea.

Exquisite Corpse

All the details had been razed
like in a blueberry barren
except for a wavy black line,
for a charred tree branch,
& above the place where the hour is folded
a super-
lative
centered as a boulder.

Only the hardiest,
bay-, boysen-, cran-
berry and the plants that sur
vive on air, on remembering no
thing, life forms made entirely of frills-lichen
age spots, trachea
of spanish moss
ball-things covered in spines or hyphens

doodles near a telephone number
for a location in the Granite State, 4810
on the nib, a mountain in slabs of cloud
from which a branch thuds
while saying the first line.

A break in the loneliness!
Begun as a drawing of a coat rack,
the lone young bull moose, stepping
out of pink brush scribble
looking for family, his antlers unpainted wood.
Bay-, boysen-, cran-

berry are from Yankee Candle.
Home-Sweet-Home,
a cross-stitch acrostic, afghan marsh
w/ macramé holders for spider plants,
knit bog, red-wing black birds
in the knots, a sandpiper
in the mirror.

Come On, Over Here

A tiny rock wall
about the size
of a toothbrush case
or a pocket ruler,
Made in Taiwan
on the painted shadow

on the underside,
a rock wall
like an ellipsis
near a pair of parenthesis
stuffed with
indian paint
brush backslashes

then (chicory) and (milkweed,
cornflowers).
Thelma Johnson (deceased),
Laverne (1969–?)
who lived in a one-room
schoolhouse
and wore eye shadow
the color of lunar moths
or prom gowns

and the spinster
Alice Hammond
in her parents' house
with a dance hall
on the second floor.

A rock wall
like a title phrase
sits on the lid of
my school desk
with its hole
for an ink jar
and a ditch for a pencil,

a This Book Belongs To:
in a child's scrawl
on a back wall
of the schoolhouse

part of the old toy set,
"A Working Farm,"
that sits in a cold, pulled light,
past the stack
of fluorescent fields
and the woods full of
underlined places

where three green children flit
faster & faster
(someone's foot
on the claw pedal)
like nymphs.

A Dream Splashed with Ropes

A dream is splashed with ropes.
Ropes are lying on the surface,
decorative ropes, descriptive sentences
from a bright yellow yarn manuscript,
cords that have slipped free of insignia
and nautical miles, roads that have slipped
from their intersections alongside tiny grass snakes
that have slipped off their skulls
from a design of gold watch fobs, tassels, gold chains:
the pattern on a splash.

      When splashes like cut-outs,
like shadows, are fit in behind certain furnishings—
behind night tables, behind the ivory headboard,
behind the his/her table lamps—when the pattern on a splash
is inserted behind the amethyst night table,
behind the headboard that's a religious city on the hill,
behind the rolling amber fields of a bedspread,
then a Dream is wheeled in, a wave charges to the left,
a wave sprayed with black knots.

What's inside the wave with drawers? Why misspell
on the manuscript of the sea? Who holds up
the one cursive word on a green schoolroom slate?
Who leads around the horses filled with rope?

A dream is splashed with ropes,
it is crisscrossed with "learning the ropes,"
"he's on the ropes," and "no strings attached,"
like an isolated wave, a wave being pulled in.

A dream, as in one's wish for the future, star-white
or a dream, sweet off-white pile, & deep inside
people you are glad to see again float
as equal signs and clover. Made to sit in a line-up,

then splayed in the hand beside the white form
that appears behind an exclamation
like a shawl of light pulled tight,
with the Incline spotted with school bricks,
the orange Slope flecked with *x*'s,
and the tear-drop
filled in with bricks.

A Dream Splashed with Ropes (2)

a dream splashed with ropes
turrets on simplicity
good to the last
drop
pre-
approved

a dream splashed with ropes
a bed ruffle on the road
the wave
with drawers
pom-pom
s of -pre

that hill gets turned
on is e-blue
the kohl-lined window
on the last barn of God

better dreamers
because of the red dream
are in
a peer-edited
swimming pool

Go-Cart Inside a Fingerprint

Miguel Ramirez, grinning, drives the golf cart inside a fingerprint
in a homespun room on paper-bag brown.
The draftsman draws and demonstrates his doing so: the line shifts
and travels, never ready to settle into a predictable design.
Down tunnel speech, pieces of sky hanging off knobs,
peaks and pyramids rising from the bare floor,
power lines strewn between jade plants on the sill.

It's not the same as walking BLOT to BLOT.
His patient 5 mph course through the loops of the room
down a braided hallway gets him sometimes to
Hal Darger, longshoreman, where clouds are written on overhead
for little girls at war and rooms are stanzaic
(this is said for my benefit). If waved on by gruff Darger,
M.R. takes a go-cart inside the hot plate,
a riding lawnmower in the pattern on a dish rag,

stands with his burro to pose beneath each π symbol
planted like grape arbors on a hill where he pauses,
looks back at A hill covered with spikes, A hill covered with other hills.
This also said for my benefit:
"I wake near the ceiling," far from doublespaced furniture,
for my friendship w/ A. G. Rezzoli, his mother cathedrals.

Incidence of Meditation Hallucinogenous with Site-Specific Factors
   Involved in Reversible Day 1

The up down, up and down of one's thoughts
dark green, gray-green, and white columns
are splices of different times and places
that a woman horsebacks through
on a carousel and across the way
sprayed-on laughter comes from a canister
labeled *Autumn in New England*

as one wades ankle-deep in water gone bright pink
through a patchwork of thyme and cilantro.
The lake is stagnant with statements,
a swizzle stick rusting flamingo leaning at one end.
One's order is up, *aji de gallina* set out on a tray
beneath the striped awning of a cloud

and like rubble from a graph fallen from the sky
the parts of a week are strewn in front of you
as well as a 3-column hedge in several places
like in a steeplechase, and the high navy Tower
of thoughts about the Future always rising,
and the stubborn taupe stubble of the past

which seen from the side become
the scent of words in the woods,
hundreds of colored puddles—
"woodsy," "fandango pink," "polynesian purple"
—that quiver, then shoot up as geysers
at 2,000 words a minute as in a state-sponsored display

of craft and artistry right before a state-sponsored display
of athleticism and technology:

the woods is a holder for a giant woman
wearing a plaid shirt & a hibiscus blossom behind her ear
in an advertisement for teeth whitening
that's about to dissolve into a series of boxes
computer-generated, like utility boxes in a landscape,
tossing herself back into a laugh
a gondola coming out of her mouth, MEN WORKING IN ROAD,
in the way in which sunset gets inserted behind trees
behind the bristle-brushes of those cell-phone towers.

"In hallways made of dashes"

1

In hallways made of dashes and hyphens
hallways that are parallels to my living and loving
because I could hear on the other side of the wall
great voices reciting in the large voices of passing subway trains
now my living is running toward my loving, shouting
what a bargain, because in a maze with blinking doors
and numbered choices (tiny clay flower pots
hiding the footnotes) and icons hibernating
at dead ends, I made my way, that little symbol I,
and could monitor my progress, 25%, 50% done, completed.
My avatar the size of a cursor and flailing its bell-bottom legs
& arms. It pauses beside cloth begonias and squirt daisies,
avoids the man reeling in footprints, the white ant that patrols a row.
Function $F^{12,}$ my little I, I jump the wall.
I make more maze by breathing, by adding code, html,
a fret design, a Greek meander which is *the figure of a labyrinth*
in linear form, by breathing.

2

I jump the wall and land on colored phrases.
I jump and land in a dumpster in the alley
because there are more forms to fill out,
a dumpster of mannequins and foam columns
I have to punch my way through giant We're #1 Hands
to get through this part. Reset, press again.
I jump and land on colored phrases
that tell me how to move like in a game of Twister,
commands, streets that tell me how to move.
In a series of streets that are directives,
because those streets had been brought inside,
in a labyrinth carved out of nostalgia, a warren of personal names,
I touch the street and more unfold beneath it,
drag my club foot onto it, my mouse hand:
in a vortex of splinters and piers, a deer path, and to an alley
of men who play backgammon off their chests
and drink a soup of nuns, my avatar is running.
Up ahead, more forms need to be filled out:
a mandala of blanks with low ceilings
and boxes color-coded with chandelier.

3

At work the next day, a few feet inside the symbol,
standing first on a stop-sign red phrase, then a tangerine warning,
looking for the yield-yellow whilst thinking to myself,
"I had heard about the legendary hand-tinted hallways of"
I knew I had to operate manually *as I sd to my friend,*
the darkness surrounds us. After the lights went out on the floor,
I peered over my wall, Kilroy Was Here.
On every screen the low-ceiling rooms of data entry,
whorl of cubicles like partitions in a fingerprint,

I had to operate manually, the way a silver ball drops
through levels of sentences, around bumpers, curbs of phrases,
spent one floor thinking over how I'd treated others
another on how I'm living my time, all the contemplation
I'd put off was in this color blown in from a faceless name:

jewel-toned halls to board rooms of chairs made by chance,
tables by weather, and guards with the acne-scarred faces
of pugs in ornamental corners. On even-numbered floors,
Insight, Awareness, Compassion. On odd-numbered,
a gold prow turned the corner just as I saw it
near the maw of the open elevator, after the copier machine.

I saw myself on a security screen as a stick figure
in a floor plan of dashes, rooms without floors, doors in ceilings.
[In the stairwell.] http: Emerging onto the roof of the building,
<waving for rescue>. *It is not the described ex*
perience of the poet that must be "resolved," but
the actual experience of the reader.

The Ceiling

A chord from the ceiling
hangs without changing
& the readers who are guests
are unsure what's next
though they agree they saw
a similar chord hanging
in the post-and-beam field
in the Pastoral and so
turn on the lights in the Tudor rehearsal space
in which the central fixture
is a clover turned into a mace
hung from a massive anchor chain:
a raft of branches,
a raft of gray arms & legs
was also spotted in the Delacroix.

                    *

A chord from the ceiling
looks like an equal sign
followed by two dots
in greenish smoke, To take two words
used earlier and repeat them
in the finale: Onward
to the professional kitchen.
The chrome dome over the appliances
is a lectern, high pulpit,
and sounding board;
under it, Emerson once gave a sermon,
on Friendship. Stylish people
are gaping at the blank

held between prongs
inside the 1976 Magnavox Console,
a handsome mahogany set,
enclosing a stadium
like the recessed amphitheater
we just passed after two master bathrooms.
Still, something may have moved
among the folding chairs in the orchestra pit
when we called out, "Is Anyone There?"
and I stubbed my foot
where a cornice angel-white
had been lowered from a paragraph.
Guests push the gate
to step out into the coda,
a balcony-sized garden:
ceiling branches.

Song-Maze

In the way a maze might appear at the corner
of someone's mouth, the multi-colored angles
that a voice is busy crocheting in a room with a pressed-tin ceiling
and the illustration of a spider plant are blocking out
things you believe someone meant you to see
besides the wicker furniture and the matriculating fern
and you feel you are a person hidden behind the couch.

The journey starts when a rope ladder is lowered
from one of his fogged-over words. Slightly elevated, like superscript
to a forest of vowels, a footnote above the man's upper lip,
the sung maze appears mid-air, a flake that doesn't go away
though dabbed at with a spinning doily or Queen Anne's lace
and this occurs beside the potted plants and the violet-flavored
sunlight that comes in a powder. It made sense. After all,

a road had emerged from the head of a woman at the top
of the room, a striped road that I roller-skated down
listening to Neil Diamond sing "They Come to America"
from an alarm-clock radio in my orange K-mart shorts
and tube socks w/ their clover-colored stripe
and by the time I reached the bottom, the 80s were done.
An ellipsis, I pull myself up by it and crawl inside.

To anyone else, it looks like a colored maze curled inside
a cloud, a fetal rainbow, this hiding in a crawl-space,
this being an apple seed in a hide-away bed, an apostrophe
in the folds of a rain cloud. Revere pans slamming
in the kitchen overhead, a Revere bell in the church tower in a window.

Entering at an angle, at the tipping point, I stand up, start walking.
I wander the rows of trees, circling certain words a couple of times,

and the man keeps singing. It's like fog singing.
His mouth a crowbar floating in a dim room,
the dune of the upper lip, his sanded-down
face anonymous. The woman on the couch has finished
her romance novel about a Zodiac. Beneath my feet are fiddleheads,
then the carved prows of waves. I start to see a colored fog
in corners of the maze, bunting,

Welcome Home. Congratulations. This song like a snow
                                        -flake
that doesn't go away. By the time I crawl out, dropping out of
                              a word,
the 90s—Clinton, Kosovo, MTV—are over.
How do I avoid circling the rows? How do I avoid the maze
that appears at the corners of everyone's lips?

A Lake in the Hand

Swimming through the indents,
and across the herringbone lake
the plane of handwriting and flourishes,
the lines of the palm, a flock of tabs
in the houndstooth sky above the lake,
I bump into a fancy signature
swimming in his lace collar and tweed coat

through the joys and concerns,
around the Rose and Thorn,
the jumps in time, gaps in knowledge
in the channels of the palm, before the school of tabs
hits the pilings, the concrete side of the dam
that is thinking about daytime television drama.
Let me say he is in a belletristic font
that he is making tremendous splashes while doing a forward crawl
and that some of the splashes look like words,

so that along with blue-rimmed pieces of water,
and red-rimmed pieces of water, a *Pardon
me* scoots forward, each wave a different color
in its wake

and I see that he is toweling off on the other shore.
A quill-like figure on a landscape of graphic design elements,
a city-state where the primary crop is cyclones
and pyramids. Whereas two score years ago, I saw
a swimmer in a claw-foot bath tub
as I was cleaning the house with my paisley.
His arm was raised like a branch

fallen on a river, the water stacked in the tub,
little "h"s on some pieces, blue rims on others,
holes to hook fingers in and transport others.
I knew he was like an Olympian
swimming at the Y, a great M in a sentence
of blue and yellow tiles

and in this document of a new freedom
a Greek key pattern fills the lake,
w/ houses that are monuments along the shore,
a flock of typed x's clatters in,
this last line with me on it like a ball
this last line zigzags
and fills the barn,
houndstooth spills into
the barn, where a small red duck paddles
innocently, in circles.

Bird Finder

The song that comes through the window
is a LONG WHITE TUBE
big enough for a full-grown man to stand up inside.
It joins the other pipes at the top of the room,
a culvert, an air duct, a fitted number 7 pipe,
a song big enough for a full-grown man to stand up inside
crossing the room like an overpass
over the gray area between *about* and *like*
and the brilliantly yellow taped-up shadow.
IN TRANSIT
is the long white song, searching for another window
to leave by, it follows the other pipes around the room
like a decoy and could go on like this for days
over upholstered hills, piles covered in stars, flowers
and in fact it does for two more stanzas

but the next line rises like a drawbridge
the whole room is tilting upward like a ramp
(the warning sound of an arm chair backing up)
(to get closer to piles of stars, gravel, road salt, extra fill).
With three lines, then only two single-spaced,
U-turn yellow bang arrow, last possible moment, the song EXITs.
The whole room is pointing N.

Bird Pattern

A red zigzag onto which is clipped a sunflower seed.
Several yards of yellow elbow with the authority.
Then a blue and white striped line twirls retro.

Carrying the sound of the highway between their beaks.
As the buildings go up and down, up down.
Moving through the laughter of the trees.

A red yellow and blue Check mark on the sky
That also appears on the foggy front of your sweater
Twirls *counterattack, blue and white neo,*

Carrying the grey, striped sound of the highway.
That red zigzag, that sunflower seed, that yellow authority,
After The Tipping Point, Robin's Break, Robin's Song,

Here's a single, says the announcer of Jazz at Night.
No, it's a Flicker and a Yellow Zinger, Charley Harper wrestling
with Audubon, says the man with the mile-long glasses.

Bird Game

In a handheld clear plastic scene with scrub trees, a bird design & a bird design spin at different rates over a barcode plant in a backyard where other games have been hidden for you under the rushes. Per hour, per second, a bebe drops through the quadrants of the mind and through pie piece rooms. A vine spiraling up a pawn. A branch or shadow like a winding slide. A shy golf club barely visible along the trunk of an ash tree in the backgammon shadows. A rotting stump with the holes of a cribbage board and spade leaves jutting behind. As black hearts run up then down a hardwood tree, a glove bird advances one square closer toward the pine-green net. Turning head-over-heels, a wing logo, green quadrant, orange u-turn, sharp kohl eye, every minute, every month. Put together the puzzle of sounds, that deflated lawn Santa. Then the dots to be filled in with the times of day and a colored maze inside a cloud. A golfer, Edward J. Whittemore III, descends from the treetops after a good drive; in an acid green splash, a woman in tennis whites mid-swing. In a hollow in a tree, an All-American slugger behind the dust of third base. To claim your prize, a pane covered with taped-together wing-tips, someone's commissioned portrait of you that leans against a tree. After a long 14 c. dotted line stem,

the coin-operated sentences.

Composition Blue No. 2 (2012)

The rectangle preens itself
near a horsehair sofa
shaped like a reclining nude
near wedges of smile
and an umlaut papaya
in a silver bowl
cut from a catalog
on a white bracket of a stand
over wheels of flowers.

The rectangle goes over & over itself
in front of a flat metallic place
where a piece of the poem
has recently been removed,
the stars unscrewed
one by one, foreclosed.

Based on the arabesques
burnt into memory by the wall
behind the cage, it must
have been a Wallace Stevens
or Mary Ruefle.
In the breakfast nook
is a cameo of Caroline Knox
over a by-line in
a newspaper, "For You,"
& the still-life on sale
circled on page 22.

Like a gray tangerine,
shards of that still-life
have fallen to one side.
You can tell the artist missed
his family, pieces of the
painting falling aside
like sections of
of gray & steam orange,
pieces of the painting
have flown away:

deep in the phonograph blossoms
of the wallpaper,
on a gold vector,
rests the née parrot.

Brite Motes

Brite motes run down the inlet
near the couch, avoid the outlet
that looks like a skull:
pegs named Paula and Astra
fill in the cove around the sofa,
the bayou under the recliner,
just as colorful pegs can hold up
the white idea in a dream,
a jungle of green asterisks
runs down a striped landslide
near the fold-away bed.
In the remodeled basement,

Who doesn't think about—Who lives among—
cards of chance behind cushions,
a question mark on every pine island,
a swing-set at the edge of a jungle,
fuzzy clouds with googly eyes
from the drop-down ceiling
that listen to "The Way We Were"
and "The Rose" and daydream about saving
up to wear Eternity on the school bus
and the petals of the
Electrolux

and shadows spilled in the basement.
In the remodeled family room,
this cavalcade:
an action figure of a woman pushing a stroller,
pushing six figures, a Morgan horse,

the Fed-Ex agent, two plastic houses,
the Hessian with a spool coming out of his side,
now a double helix, on the astro-turf,
a board game in which I live in a mote with a turret,
shag carpet on each island,
on each island a reading lamp
the shadow under a pine tree: a spotlight.

A Strip of Woods at the Back of the Mind

Glued-on trees alternating with
strips of bricks and little pieces of song
taped up everywhere as green and pink diamonds

in a woods in a box when the room of the mind
has an easy chair and 3 large trees.
A 3-sided woods with a divan at the back,

an argyle of bird song on top
of a syncopation of stapled trees,
concrete strips and birches tacked up

for *reflection, digression, analysis*
if the room in the mind means
3 large people conferring in a box of woods

with a love seat out front.
Bands of fluorescence and poplar
and a tempo of tacked-up trees

a needlepoint of bird song, home-sweet-home,
where a sapling on an end table is lit
stage right beside the wicker chair

as well as the leather chair in the boxed woods.
A gray-haired woman sits on the floor
to read stacks of old journals out of a crate,

a flaxen girl in a Scotch-plaid holiday dress
who rolls in stage left.
Pulses of gold and lamé trees in French

and a disco ball in the boxed-in woods,
if the many-roomed mind comes with a futon.
The off-kilter, out-of-sync,

the irregular pace of, the size 3 of, until

a (Do Not) diagonal across the mountain range
at the back of the mind, sound-split poles, stubs
but *glued-on, syncopation, many stapled, love lit:*

one by one, the leaves again taped up.

Klee Carpets

It was like being asked to wash down a Paul Klee.
A border of rhythmic rooms around the hour,
My daughter lost in pastel cities at two years, then three.

For a $25 rental fee,
A rainbow sentence appears on the floor.
It was like being asked to wash down a Paul Klee

To steam-clean carpets from my in-laws' travels:
Times Square, Red Square, Town Oval, Leaning Tower.
My daughter is running ahead in squares of two years, then three.

For $25, I can pick up the cuticle of the moon, the pointed feet
Dashing into the scene, my tall daughter says, A city on the floor!
It was like being asked to wash down a Paul Klee.

. . . and the pointed feet, the rush to the hospital, the travail.
This rainbow city that starts with an inflatable funhouse A,
My daughter, missing, in a watercolor city for two years, then three

Until I find her in an A-frame house in Seraph font.
Exiting the city, she is quietly Narkism in my arms.
Each fringe a mile. The moon is what she calls a dirty moon.

It was like being asked to wash down a Paul Klee.
My daughter found in square cities at two years, then three.

Outsider Art

He stops at a neologism
       at a spot he hasn't worked on

in years, near a grove of popsicle sticks
saved from Vacation Bible School
in an autobiography written in bumper stickers

from which a plagiarized Bengal tiger
leaps at a self-portrait of Rembrandt.

"I'm Tony the Tiger," he says to
a Chock-full-o'Nuts can
that captures a drawing of rain

coming in through a yellow tarp.
Above a vintage Coca-Cola machine
he's drawn marble scalloping
but likes his stenciling just as well.

Night shift. His Medusa mop in a corner
for cleaning up what he thinks

of as a flock of business cards
in the honeycomb under the stadium
        and the hotel beside it,
other people's desires slamming
against the wall as colored lights
like ice in the ice maker.

Potholes are in the fluorescent light.

He uses a fat blue crayon to BACK UP
                WIDE LOAD

It's like driving between fields of gray tulips
to reach the all-nite diner where Marilyn
and James Dean wait on stools for
his buddy never back from Vietnam
                                who died in
the 1918 flu epidemic.

If only he could get to the spot
where they only ever use new words.

Lawn Ornaments, Robins, Ode to Clocks

The musical sentences
of soft blue and orange letters
   blow across the yard
set in brackets, set in early summer,
      with the lawn clock
registering 4:56 AM

in different combinations
      the same seven letters
appear like soap bubbles
on stems and blades, on prefixes or stems
      and wobble in the breeze
forming a word purely by chance
      near the Hello Kitty alarm clock. Letters

poured out of tubes for song,
      laid six across
like logs in the sky,
then strung out in all caps
      on ellipses of humidity
on tiny chains between thoughts.
When I see the actual birds,
      they seem on mute
         in the wood-fringed yard.
Near the unique date and time
on the rolling clock, the water clock,

a robin pretends to be a lawn ornament.
He has an orange sticker on his chest.
The lawn swells in word count

scattering phrases on twigs
around the World Clock, GMT,
for the lawn-care guys to pick up,

these inflatable letters,
        with the children back in school,
cling to the poplar trees
        with leaves taped on one by one,
to the dwarf fruit trees
        never meant to produce
anything.
                Replaced by
more and more transparent letters,
the song is fall-colored,
then winter-colored,
and the lyre clock
is mostly a Mystery (shelf) model.

Bird Insert

To be part of the pack, that cloud of ducts at the ceiling, the white line of song goes to different lengths, trying on one screw-on phrase after another, right at the preposition, at the chevron-, spade-, cross-shaped preposition. It tries on cardinal and a waxy cornflower blue that looks like a crayon mark that's taken a swipe across the room and even tries seagull, but to others it still looks hard, white, and unripe. Its happiest stretch is when it passed under some deep song after neon song and a hum 3" in diameter and was able to run alongside it, *and thus raise any line of this poem like a windshield-wiper or a drawbridge.* It's choking out the moment with its lines, its afghan marsh, its crochet bog, its "This is what it comes to" and "By all means." And when the gang of pipes starts taking turns, swooping down to hook one-by-one flowers to their own ends, This is what it comes to: it does the same.

Winter Wonder World

Boxes are filled with emotion,
moving boxes, boxes moving inside boxes,
filled with a moving spirit,
boxes filled with other boxes
ivory on beige, white on white,
a paragraph lined with snow

into which dangle the black stocking legs
thin as twigs, the sharp-eyed feelings,
the ornate blue, white and gray hood.
You did what??? shoots out
like a branch, and *What did you do*
with the snow, you fool

Eye-gleam or thawing.
In the paragraph padded with snow
more birds drop down as ornaments
with glitzy snowflakes from the Dollar Store:

the sound of snow yanked off a metal roof
the wet red smell of a wool mitten with a snowflake design
the crunch of your Star Wars boots in the woods ™
are hanging on branches, hanging on black lashes.

Flora to Fauna

In a room is a silken pile of the world's flowers, none repeated twice and without stems, leaves, supporting attachments, words without their stems. Because the mind likes categories, it makes dunes of golden upholstery, basalt bolsters. It imagines a floral pattern and bird song swooping down to liberate the flowers, escorting each tremble out of the repetition, that the flowers are a typed color. The song is hard, white, unripe. A pack of pipes races around the top of the room, and the tube of bird song tags behind them as they are diving down to hook, one-by-one they attach screw-on flowers to their own ends: the day-glo lily, the apple blossom, the rose, the midnight tulip, and ride around with it for awhile. It makes no difference that this turns the ceiling into a cloud of pathways, then a storm sky of twists and turns, or that they are treating it as a speedway. Atop the roof, a weathervane, made with a black arrow connecting two birds of prey, turns.

The floor littered now with white blossoms.
The song is like a hard white unripe strawberry.

The Coil

Rushing thru/to
the knot and the snarl,
the concentric circle, the cul de sac
with a doorless house
and the maze inside a cloud.
Rushing thru/to the knot and the soul,
to the one-leaf tree, a single black wing
on the horizon outside an industrial park. The road has given up,
the street is pinned up, the line has shed its skin,
the path up and died, a pine tree is blinking
like a cursor and the last ¼ mile is in a drawer.

Backing up, I feel the curve of this phrase,
feel the brick-red phrase, the no and the yes, the terracotta curve,
following this line for several typed yards,
feeling my way along the walls, I come across
a sudden collection of details pooling
against the low wall of a dead end, at a blinking door:
bags in trees, coins of faces, MP3 players, cover art, umbrellas. Ice floes
of Explorer, Expedition, Everest, Escape,
Pathway, Journey, Territory, Path Finder, and Trail Blazer
and (Bienvenue) and (If You Lived Here).

An excavation, ½ an industrial park, a symbolic house
is at the rest stop, a house with painted-on doors,
the long porch a façade. Drivers carry flares
in their mouths, the woman to my right waters
houseplants on her passenger side,
I sit listening to tin foliage, a man in his future
steps off an escalator, levitates above a subway platform
with his briefcase of lint—his hyphen, color, suitcase

—and a sleeping toddler swirls
in an eddy, a cul de sac.

On foot, I follow the rusty splashes
of the poem on the walls, the dripping sound,
the large voices passing on the other side like trains,
the corroding door to a misspelled passage.
I stop short in my tracks: hibernating icons
are in piles in every corner, and the tiny ouroboroi
are stirring, the Don't Tread on Me
is stirring, the rattler, superscript dragons,
the treaty of the anaconda,
a sentence that is biting its own tail,

a sentence that swallowed another sentence.
We tug and tug at the hose
coming from underground.
We tug and tug and we bend over and pull
at this stub coming out of the ground.
We pull to get to our golden house
our house of golden in a subdivision,
a dale of one-leaf trees, pulling
at the sentence sleeping at the end, the one in which
the walls of the poem are moving, muscular walls
contracting the splash-pattern of words,

a Toyota Corolla & ¼ of a shopping mall,
a tollbooth and the blinking tree
slide past on lengths of phrases, scattering
the packs, colonies, swarms, flocks,
the congress, troop, gang, congregation,
the mob, cast, brood, nest,
school, company, bevy, horde and covey,
all great & small to the sound of a traffic helicopter.

Price

In the circle of my inspection
which is an eyelet from a wave
that has the lace taken off a splash,
while the hour has been hole-punched,
& a yellow measuring tape
of forsythia is draped across the mountain,

I see the price, the clove carpet,
the scarlet sticker, the maroon shadow.
I am either ice fishing at a séance,
or interviewing for a job,
having lunch with my boss in her office.
On the table is a spike, a peak, a crest

a chart draped like a red net
on the top of a water mountain.
Her assistant comes in
wearing a tie with cherry blossoms
and holding a plate of deductibles,
olive and black shadows under a chicken breast.

While the hour has been hole-punched,
a single wave is on the coffee table,
& garlands of pastel highways
& yellow police tape are draped
across this water mountain, I see the price,
smoke in the ice cubes,

and that a braided rug lies under the conversation
near the underlined parts of the room,
and that certain things are rising
out of the floor. A girl with bee's lips,
crystals tinged w/ exhaustion,
a bottle filled with striped smoke,

a bobbing trapezoid—
I tamp them down with my heel.
In the coffee table book about waves,
cobalt and lacquered layers dip   dip
blue shellac depths
over men in a bread basket of a boat.

When her assistant appears on the horizon,
his tie speaks, "A mountain
covered with one hundred waves,
or a wave with 100 mountains on it."
The men in an open boat cower
beneath the yellow-clawed wave,

master, I tamp it down with my heel,
with my dot, with this speck.
While having lunch with my boss,
I see my Honda in the parking lot
rising,   rising
A single wave, a −whelm, on the coffee table.

Tassel

The tassel on that thought,
the grommet at one end of the lake,
the drop on a Norwegian pine,

a drop filled in with bricks
tipping the whole gloomy tree in its favor.
The tassel on that thought

is larger than the thought.
The anvil-shaped pause,
a football-shaped indent,

a laugh wrapped in foil,
a hiccup embossed in leather:
I am wrapping gifts for all

the people to whom I'm fastened.
The underline that precedes
the house, the three small houses set

atop a lake. An eyelet at the other end.
Here comes the snowmobile patrol.
The tassel on that thought:

Its color is straight from the bottle.
The tassel is a lioness who insists
on accompanying you down

the PVBLIC stairs
while carrying a wheat blade for a spear.
To be reincarnated as the couch.

Part the curtains along the shore,
the heavy drapery of pines,
a fleck caving in, a smirk left

in a landscape, a national attraction:
kitten batting at a tassel of sky,
a tassel of rain.

Hallucinogenous Bullfighter, 1970

The heart is a bull
pawing at orange peels,
sunset
a strobe knife in his head.
Memory floods
in anger.
The blood flies
who teased him are now tigers.
This end came out of nowhere
like a flame,
courtship a ringing sadness
in which a man grew old
in one night.
Was the fight always so
vacant?
The little lad, the autobiographer
in sailor's suit, always
here with the camera of
night?
Was there ever a rope of love
at the side of the coliseum?
And who is throwing
the roses, the roses
the lit roses & the hot burners
to the victorious pain
in his chest?

The Page-Dream

Across the page-dream
moves a paper clip swan.
I've a blue eye on my finger
—w/ three inky lashes—
and a corn maze on my palm.

The page-dream is white-hot
all the details razed
I've a brown eye on my finger
and a five-sided
fort in my palm

though not this wavy line,
a charred branch.
Where the love line
meets the Apollo line
a cuticle of a boat

travels down homemade map
on my hand, passing swan boats
and duck boats, a family of Sea Monkeys
—father goes by name Poseidon—
waiting to move into a dorm!

The page-dream, a white-hot smell.
We move by association
across the psychic-page,
See Fig. 2. Fold by fold.
A shout goes up:

One side is loose, boys!
Ditties, sea chantey, sequins, and scales,
Footnote in Psychology 100
and in Palmistry 101,
the paper clip swan.

At different stations,
Near floating crosses,
a family of sea monsters
waits in ambush on sea-foam
mattresses taken from the dorm

moves a psychic swan.
A crescent on an index finger,
means travel to the Crescent City.
I don't remember much of high school
and even less of college, white song.

Ingredients

Grooved water
menthol, diethyl 2
Red Lake, the flavoring
of the days of the week,
values.

Grooved water,
the three red dots
that appear in a premonition
over a lake at night,
argyle pond,
diced marsh.

I was single and visiting my sister at the lake.
Everyone asleep, the hammocks sleeping in the trees
the grill cold, a tube sock of my nephew on the floor.
I did not know if I ever would become a mother.
I was in my early thirties: at the three red numbers of the alarm clock,
I began rowing

passing the hose of a loon
on her concentric nest
in the haz-mat water,
heading to the sallow island,
the butter island
with the three pines
that were questions.

Sorbic Acid (Nightmare Extract)
Benzyl Alcohol

Honey (Honey) in sepia,
lake with handles,
pond with slits.

Grooved water
that can kill you if you hold
onto it too long,

clutching at rusting reeds
as you pass to change
the pitch, volume,
or pacing.

We were all little figures
skating above the vast watery
surface of her, the vast written surface.
Or my Dad drove,
steering the 1968 honeymoon
car on two planks set over the bluest
tropical ocean.

Going over and over
the same spot, making miracles
and concentric circles,
a broken ice pattern
for a tabletop.

The Neighbors

Raj and Denis live with each other near the eaten fence.
Raj is a diamond-backed, Denis has a white splash on his face
like the one on my fountain pen which is a killer whale.
A chord from Beethoven is suspended in the sky
over the sulky fields near the Orchard View housing development.
It looks like a pile of spikes, rays & religious thoughts of a saint,
the type of chandelier you wouldn't want to pass over you
as you dined at the long table. Back and forth
it grills you, some sort of Argonaut
while people put spoons into a terrific vichyssoise.
We're new to the neighborhood, and when Raj comes to the door
he is holding a plate of argyle cookies.
Pieface and Pickaxe one cul de sac over,
Barb and Lance Speer, both palominos, what's up with them?
-a gated community, a tennis court above the lace
            at the bottom of my 17th-century porcelain skirt.
It always looks so wet and sad here, like a kitten out in the rain
who has lost his home, and he goes from door to door
each one blocked by an impressive puddle, and people think
in this illustration that the kitten is saying "mitten,"
precisely how I am feeling. Denis digs out his oboe.
-shows us a drip painting done in calcium of his daughters
who wear software necklaces and were lost sometime during
    Reconstruction.
On the way to the cinema of obstructions, in our Bismarck Saab,
my husband says, Relax,
-emphasis on "ax"
don't worry about it, they're only horses right after the dissolving fence.

Gift Basket

W/ contrails for handles
& a face in the weaving
59¢ a blurry stamp on the sky
clouds from the back of the cooler
on sky the color of the word *next*,
and a white ampersand
new baby new house new job,
it's a basket that holds white asterisks,
baby's breath, a vertical horizon,
and it also carries this thought:
"Flowers—to keep
the Eyes—from going awkward"
(Emily Dickinson)
right over the gaudy applause
of pansies the patriotic applause
of petunias in the driveway.
This gift basket,
while I am off shopping
at Market Basket,
swings its woven face
over the squiggle of oaks
over deep-set dirt in the folds
of the white flowers
said often, thank you and okay,
over the word *over*
over This Book Belongs To,
over baby's first book,
the new face swings
above the new house.

Spring Version

Engineers are using Scotch tape
and slide rulers to tape up,
among school pennants like wind socks,
the fuzzy pastels of bird song
but mostly girls' names   opal
to the illustrations of short trees;

they parachute frangipani
and Juicy Fruit
and open while ascending.

To be interested in
the changing seasons is a happier state
than to be hopelessly
in love with spring.
—George Santayana.

.

.

.

.

-escent.

Oh, yes, in the yellow yard,
the soft tubular words—
boas of pollen
and Slinky-s of bangles
are level on the air—
flounces of drawn-out answers
descend mid-way and open

passing tiny notes on folded paper.
Splashes of buildings,
some more happy than others
dropping -escent.

Bob's Keys to the Kingdom

The large man-shaped key
in hunter orange contact paper
is walking out of a limerick
with a fleur-de-lys in a kimono
made from an origami of springtime

and both are inserted into a landscape
with a wrench-shaped sky.
You can get them made
at your hardware store
for around 59¢.

They are friends with all
the colors of nail polish,
"Private Viewing," "Indeed," "The Taxpayer,"
the patina of others' lives:
"Sage green really is a marvelous
color for a baby," as they stroll
around the splish-splash
of the fountain tiled with the names
of boys from Massachusetts and Delaware.

There are pliers but also hunters
in all the different ways to open a landscape.
But the maple leaf with a pointer in a language lesson:
Instructor! The leaf sighs
                because it is happy to be an instructor
in a Berlitz language book
carrying an exclamation mark like a pointer
in all the different ways to open a landscape.

Into the Diurnal Proofing Oven

Into the Diurnal Proofing Oven
goes the embossed rock wall
on the calling card,
the wet rock wall
on the business card

then the test strips
with bands of
purple September
and yellow October,

the purple scent
of wild grapes
beside waterproof yellow
in a scratch 'n sniff moment

when the most real
seems the most artificial.

*

Into the Diurnal Proofing Oven
with the trademark of Hour
and Every Minute
and tidings from a Seal of Approval

passes the purple superlative
next to the asterisk-leaf,
goes the glove left on the rock wall.

Making a royal crest in the air,
a medieval stained-glass window
celebrates Saint Steve:
a hand of grapes
& an empty stainless
steel glove. A Shrinky Dink.

Q & A

You leapt over the rock wall. Yes, repeatedly.
You were frequently on the answer side,
Under the glossy sky. Yes.
The thunderstorm that leaves more answers on
The ground. Copies of answers across the fields,
upside-down answers under the horse chestnut. Leaping man,
You were the left flame and the right flame,
the sterling wall, the pewter wall,
Leaping man: the row of 14-carat lights on my finger. Yes,
We've already discussed that.
I ate the bread, and I ate the fire you packed.
You did. And yet I never found you
no matter how hard I looked
despite the pleas that planted themselves in my mouth
my mouth that went round and round.
Sir, there are twenty-one more questions.
Would that be alright? In what sense.
Seven of them are mahogany, two are teak,
and one in the ivory you requested, you son of a bitch.
I hear the breeze picking up over the meditation music, do you?
How did you slap on all those shadows, all that light?

Yard Sale

On a tarp over the beige grass,
the circled parts of the world

have been set out: The Focus, the Zoom-In,
the circled parts of the ground

the ones that say "That's All Folks!"
that telescope in and out.

In the boggy woods of swamp maples
near a swing set a boxed set of cat tails

is underlined twice, for emphasis.
It's the underline that has preceded me

for days like a forward shadow
when I pursued the DayGlo kettle,

the highlighted phone. Near the upturned corner
of the yard, a puzzle of sounds &

an Interrobang:
the fly I accidentally killed this morning

is walking straight back at me
across the shag carpet.

NOTES

"Deconstructing New England" contains material from Robert M. Thorson, *Stone by Stone,* as well as light paraphrases of Robert Frost and E. B. White.

"Surveillance meteor" is dedicated to Franz Wright.

The Bird Series is based on the illustrations of Charley Harper.

"Go-Cart Inside a Fingerprint" contains material from the Museum of American Folk Art, *Self-Taught Artists of the 20th Century.*

"In hallways made of dashes" contains material from Rumi, Karl Kerenyi, *Dionysus: Archetypal Image of Indestructible Life,* Robert Creeley, and Barbara Hernnstein Smith, *Poetic Closure: A Study of How Poems End.*

"Hallucinogenous Bullfighter, 1970" is based on Salvador Dali's painting of that title. I want to thank Tania Pryputniewicz for restoring this poem to me—reminding me that I had written it years before.

ACKNOWLEDGEMENTS

"Bird Saver" and "Surveillance meteor" in *New American Writing*; "Ingredients" in *Yew Journal*; "Lilacs" in the *Denver Quarterly*; "The Lottery of Winged Leaves," "Klee Carpets," "Gift Basket," "Brite Motes," "Bath Toys Sit in the Description," and "Bob's Keys to the Kingdom" in the *Chariton Review*; "Oh, Massachusetts" in *The Fertile Source*; "A Dream Splashed with Ropes" and "A Dream Splashed with Ropes (2)" in *Volt*.

IOWA POETRY PRIZE AND
EDWIN FORD PIPER POETRY AWARD WINNERS

1987   Elton Glaser, *Tropical Depressions*
        Michael Pettit, *Cardinal Points*

1988   Bill Knott, *Outremer*
        Mary Ruefle, *The Adamant*

1989   Conrad Hilberry, *Sorting the Smoke*
        Terese Svoboda, *Laughing Africa*

1990   Philip Dacey, *Night Shift at the Crucifix Factory*
        Lynda Hull, *Star Ledger*

1991   Greg Pape, *Sunflower Facing the Sun*
        Walter Pavlich, *Running near the End of the World*

1992   Lola Haskins, *Hunger*
        Katherine Soniat, *A Shared Life*

1993   Tom Andrews, *The Hemophiliac's Motorcycle*
        Michael Heffernan, *Love's Answer*
        John Wood, *In Primary Light*

1994   James McKean, *Tree of Heaven*
        Bin Ramke, *Massacre of the Innocents*
        Ed Roberson, *Voices Cast Out to Talk Us In*

1995   Ralph Burns, *Swamp Candles*
        Maureen Seaton, *Furious Cooking*

1996   Pamela Alexander, *Inland*
        Gary Gildner, *The Bunker in the Parsley Fields*
        John Wood, *The Gates of the Elect Kingdom*

1997   Brendan Galvin, *Hotel Malabar*
        Leslie Ullman, *Slow Work through Sand*

1998   Kathleen Peirce, *The Oval Hour*
        Bin Ramke, *Wake*
        Cole Swensen, *Try*

1999   Larissa Szporluk, *Isolato*
        Liz Waldner, *A Point Is That Which Has No Part*

2000   Mary Leader, *The Penultimate Suitor*

2001   Joanna Goodman, *Trace of One*
        Karen Volkman, *Spar*

2002   Lesle Lewis, *Small Boat*
        Peter Jay Shippy, *Thieves' Latin*

2003   Michele Glazer, *Aggregate of Disturbances*
        Dainis Hazners, *(some of) The Adventures of Carlyle,
            My Imaginary Friend*

2004   Megan Johnson, *The Waiting*
        Susan Wheeler, *Ledger*

2005   Emily Rosko, *Raw Goods Inventory*
        Joshua Marie Wilkinson, *Lug Your Careless Body
            out of the Careful Dusk*

2006   Elizabeth Hughey, *Sunday Houses the Sunday House*
        Sarah Vap, *American Spikenard*

2008   Andrew Michael Roberts, *something has to happen next*
        Zach Savich, *Full Catastrophe Living*

2009   Samuel Amadon, *Like a Sea*
        Molly Brodak, *A Little Middle of the Night*